10 GREAT SHORT STORIES

MORAL NEEDED IN EVERYDAY LIFE

ARKADEEP KUNDU

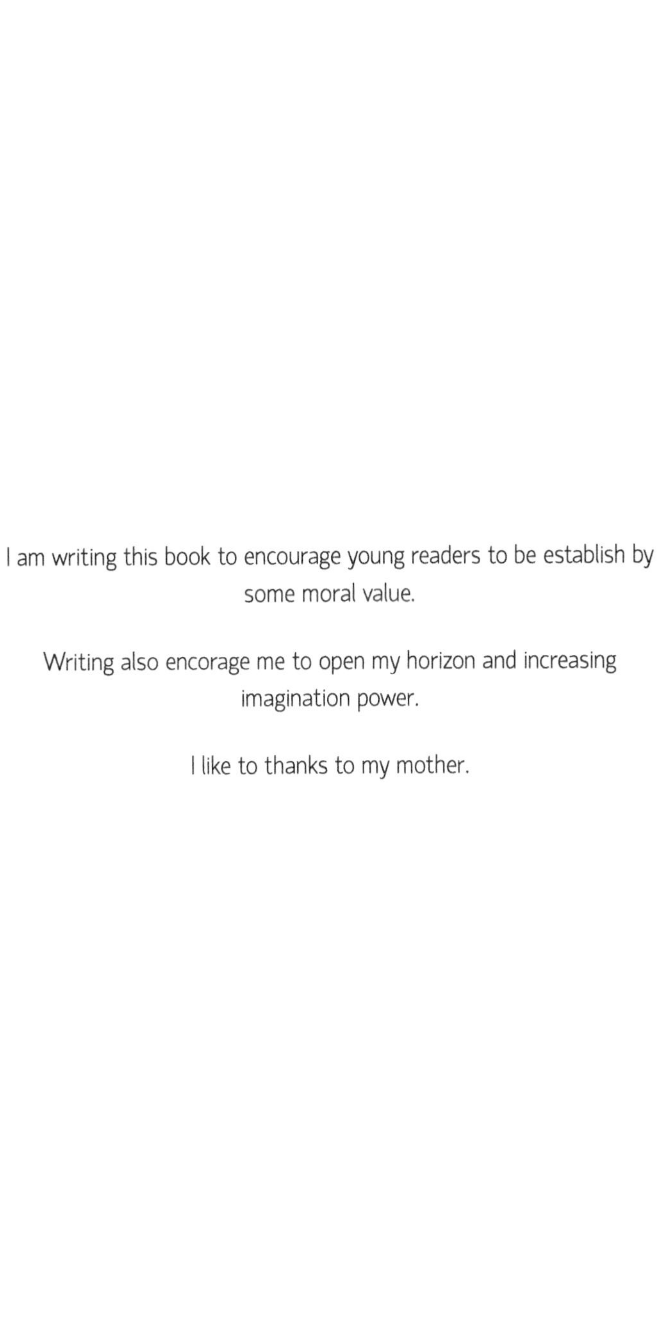

I am writing this book to encourage young readers to be establish by some moral value.

Writing also encorage me to open my horizon and increasing imagination power.

I like to thanks to my mother.

Contents

Foreword

These book is about fiction and it describes about the moral values needed tp be establish in our everyday life and continue to make every child a responsible human in thier future life.

Preface

I myself **Arkadeep Kundu** is writing these to be more encoraging and motivating.

Acknowledgements

Inspired by **RK Narayana** and many other short stories writers

CHAPTER ONE

A FOURTY-LEGGED CREATURE

Quite a time ago there was a village named Pitampad. On the mid of autumn, a group of children where playing in the village field.

Suddenly they saw and felt that the land was shaking and every children and even the people that were surrounding the field were also extremly afraid. So children left the field at first and after that everyone left the fiel with their heart ached with fear.

Then suddenly they saw a creature erupted from the field and everybody surrounding the field was afraid that earthquake was coming. After sometimes they saw a strange looking creature is erupting from underground the field. The villagers were standstill like dry wood.

Suddenly a brave man named Kishan who works in army have a gun in his hand at the time.

He was near it but he fought that creature with courage by firing more than 70 bullets without being afraid and thus he killed that creature.

He thus was known for his bravery and courage.

Moral - Courage to be known.

CHAPTER TWO

Homeless to Singer

On 80's there was a boy named Rohit Sheeren who was suffering from bit schizophrenia and became bit autistic at the toddler age of 3. He has a brother and two elder sisters they have good bonding. For this condition everyone from his siblings to his family and friends used to teased him and make fun of him.

So he was very afraid and tensed and loose confidence all the times in a day.

He is now 15 but left his school due to uncontrollabe teasing and lack of help from the teachers.

That autism not only affect him mentally but also physically and as days were going he was becoming weaker and weaker.

So Rohit's parents and siblings thrown him out from his house one day and now he became homeless.

Due to this he saw that many beggars were singing aqnd so he also thought to beg day and night. He also begged everyday and then collect all the money to bought a string harp.

As everyone on that locality were Rohit use to sing began to know him.

So one day a music producer was passing through that footpath and after seeing him the music producer have grabbed him and gave an offer for singing as he was very impressed by his singing.

This is how the journey for become a singer began to take place and now he is happy to be part of it.

An Unknown Mysterious Cabin

Here a place name Janakganj have a vast huge field. On the opposite side of the field near a tea shop there was a cabin.

At night near the cabin some unwanted feary noises used to echoed all around and everyone was afraid by that noise.

People used to get extremly afraid and they used to avoid the surrounding.

No one even dear to roam around the cabin as everyone was afraid of it.

It is tremendously dangerous for everyone around.

Only Venkat have the guts as he was least afraid of all the ghostly talk and figure areound that used to roam near the cabin.

So despite being afraid he fought with all his mental and physical strength and after he won against the fear of ghost and with heart full of courage he opened the cabin with utmost gut and bravery.

Venkat break open the lock and it was very difficult for him to open it.

After opening the cabin he saw various old and expensive potraits were being there inside and due to vacuum inside and some metallic things inside the noise used to flank open and so people used to afraid of it.

There was also expensive crockeries present inside the cabin.

Moral : We need to cultivate courage after knowing it.

Hiking In Ayodhya Hill

Ayodhya Hill is the hill located at Purulia,West Bengal,India and it is a very well known camping and trekking side. About two months ago in October, Shivesh went to hiking with his good friends named Sunil, Sanjoy, Anil and Amrit.

They boarded the train by taking all trekking gears to Purulia to get into Ayodhya Hills at 5a.m in the morning and everyone was immensely excited.

After boarding the train all were tremendously excited and within five hours they reached Purulia.

At their they have breakfast and hired a car to visit Ayodhya Hills.

After reaching Ayodhya Hill everyone placed their tent and ready for camping.

Near the base of the hill they had their lunch and then set up for trekking.

After going halfway through the hill with the help of trekking gear Anil and Amrit were afraid to climb the whole peak themselves as they were feeling clumsy and feeling vomiting and exhausted and immensely tried and worned up on that moment.

So with the help of rope and three other friends named Sunil, Sanjoy and Shivesh they hold the rope tight fisted and not loose their will ,hope and confidence.

The hiked took them for more than three and half hour and everyone was excited and feeling wounderful around.

After rising at the tip of the peak Ayodhya Hill they felt very proud after touching the peak and the view of the sunset was quite awesome for them.

The sunset was very gift for their trek....

Moral of the Story: A friend in need is a friend in-deed.

CHAPTER FIVE

An Incredible Fox

Once upon a time there was a fox in Nallamalla forest. He is very cunning and a clever fox and that forest is filled with tigers.

One day while the fox was going to have deer for his lunch but the tiger was thirsty and the same time with it.

So the fox thought not to let the tiger to hunt for the deer for it's dinner.

So he here arranged by putting leftover twigs near the deer and making a huge hole so that tiger could not succeed to catch the deer.

By having this as a plan the fox's mission was successful and he was happy.

The thing happened as it was told and the fox thought about it.

This is how the fox win the deer to have food for it's lunch.

CHAPTER SIX

Desperation for Money

A boy named John was aged 18 and he recently passed out from his school. He is now 18 so he can have an individual bank account of his own and he has the hobby of owning a credit card by his name.

On that particular day after passing his higher secondary exam John visited a bank nearest to his house.

As he was unaware that for creating an account we need identity documents such as Voter Card, Aadhar Card and PAN Card.

On that individual day he totally blotted out for bringing those documents ans so account creation was pending. On the next day he created his account fully and then order for a credit card and within a span of 15 days he got his credit card. He has now become desperate about money and thought to buy anything he needed.

That credit card has a limit of Rs1000 a month.

But John spend beyond that amount to buy accessories   like shirt,shoes,headphones,microphones   and many other to fulfil his want.

Now, his wants exceeds his need in a ratio of 2:1 and he relentlessly spend buy useless things to fulfil his gratification and FOMO(FEAR OF MISSING OUT).

John's credit card bill was half-yearly and he do not track his spending and how his unnecessary desperation of money began to develop.

That useless desperation was craving him from inside but it seems from outside that he is becoming confident and self-dependent.

When the time of paying his credit card bill came he have lack of money and he more money to spend his card monthly bills. This is how he has been drowned in the sea of debts as a debt-trap cycle due to massive desperation of money.

So, he now need to sell his necessary equipments to pay the credit card bill.

That how, desperation kill a man the real purpose in his life.

CHAPTER SEVEN

A man with Hubris

Once upon a time there was a man named Mikhael and he was home homeless.

He had the habit of buying lottery tickets every week.

So after buying the ticket he was excited and then he thought he will win the lottery jackpot.

After the result he saw that he won the lottery and was super-excited.

He won a lottery of $2million and was excited and filled himseld with hubris.

After that he bought a mansion and 3 fancy cars and then he used to have camlavish lifestyle calling all off his friends and showing his wealth in an unassuming manner.

Everyone surrounding him was enjoying every bits of his earning.

A real time came and he need to face the harsh truth and so nobody was their areounfd him when he lost all his money and went bankrupts due to his prideness of having money.

Atlast the money didn't protect him and that was the problem we need to face in these harsh world.

After that he filed bankruptcy and then become homeless again.

Moral:: Immense proud is bad for our both inner and outer peace.

Faking A Death

Some years ago there was a man named Surinder from border town of Ferozepur in Punjab,India.

Due to great heroine production and distribution of drugs like cocaine and heroine in Pakistan everyone was addicted to drug. So that neverending problems also affects many border states like Haryana, Rajasthan, Punjab, Kashmir and especially Punjab is most affected.

He was extremly addicted to drug like cocaine and morphine and that is killing him from inside.

One day while having drugs in the field with his friends and so all of them where caught except Surinder.

He totally faked his death as such a great pace and that police department failed to recognize him that he was pretending to do that to save himself.

After that time police used to keep an eye on him everyday 24 hours.

Police used to toiled around his house. At last he was caught as police department thought he will came to his home even once a while.

But after a week he was caught by a mob of 7 polices it was difficult for them to caught him due to his unlimited uncountable restlesssnessof Surinder due to unlimited consumption of illegal superaddicted drugs.

Surinder thought he was very clever but atlast he was being caught at midnight without any hesitation and mistakes by the team.

Caring Brothers

Arun and Varun are two brothers. There bondings are so strong that mentally or by imagination it seems that they are connected by each other's body parts.

Whenever Varun is in need Arun is always where it is good time, better time , bad time or the worst time.

Same thing also goes similar for Arun as there bond is everlasting.

One day when Arun was travelling from his home to his home to his office he met with an accident.

The accident occurs due to the careless of a mini-truck driver as the driver was there to open the door of his truck.

Arun was in hurry and he carelessly and without noticing his baike went dashed against the truck's door and so he slipped away from his bike and afterwhile both off his leg start bleeding.

On that police arrested the police arrested the truck driver and called an ambulance to take him to the nearest hospital for treatment.

After that despite being in immense pain he called his elder brother Varun and he was there right within an hour from his office.

From going to the hospital to taking Arun to his house, Varun have done everything.

He also done everything from buying medicince to take care off Arun after that without any obstacle and hesitation.

When Arun was at home Varun care about him Selflessly without any problem.

MORAL :: A brother indeed is always a brother indeed.

CHAPTER TEN

The brave boy

A few years ago a baby boy Suresh was swimming with all his friends in his

village. They were immensely enjoying swimming from one part of the pond to another without any fear.

But suddenly due to heavy breeze a strong and the breeze was so strong that it was blowing and the made the water looked like it has jumped all along the way.

So , Suresh could not control his body step and maintaing equilibrium and so extra water gulped down his body and he then lost his control and drowned.

Nobody near the pond have the guts to save Suresh but only Venkatesh have the guts and so he dip into the pond with utmost courage and bravery and so he did not feel any sense and without bothering anything round him and motto to save Suresh.

Venkatesh search for him all across the pond and fond Suresh at the last norteast corner of the pond.

So without being afraid he picked him up and then showed along the path and took him on the bank.

After pressing near the ribcage of Suresh, Venkat eliminate the water fro his body and thus is how he was being saved.

At last every villagers praised Suresh with utmost care for his corage and bravery.

THE WRITING IS THEIR TO DEVELOP SOME MORAL
VALUES..

www.ingramcontent.com/pod-product-compliance
Lightning Source LLC
Chambersburg PA
CBHW021813150726
47989CB00004B/1916